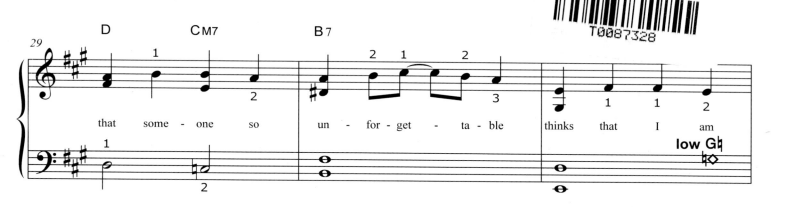

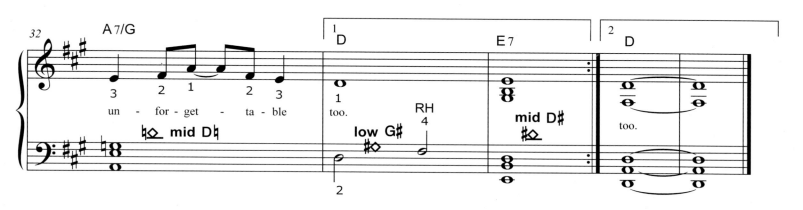

3

Unforgettable
for lever harps tuned to flats

Words and music by IRVING GORDON
Arranged for harp by SYLVIA WOODS

Set your sharping levers for the key signature, and then re-set the levers shown above.
The lever changes in measures 2 and 31 should be made as late in the measure as possible.
Repeated melody notes with no fingerings listed may be played with either finger 1 or 2.

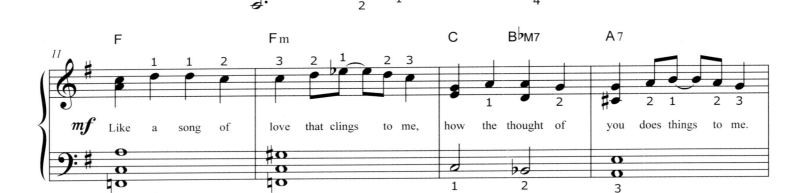

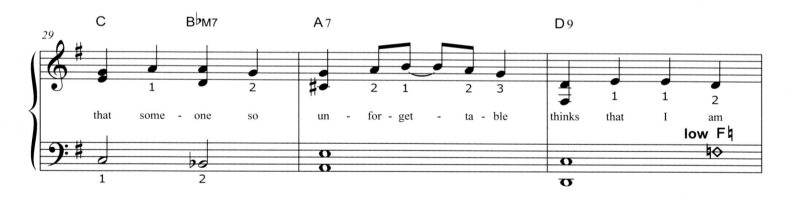

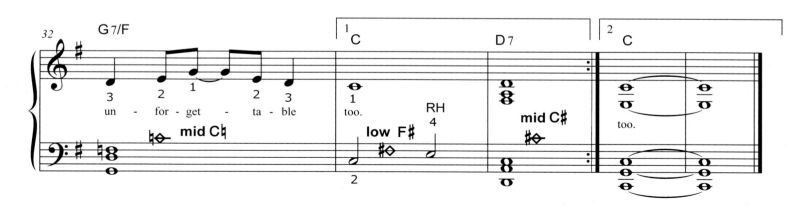

5

Unforgettable
for pedal harps

Repeated melody notes with no fingerings listed may be played with either finger 1 or 2.

Words and music by IRVING GORDON
Arranged for harp by SYLVIA WOODS

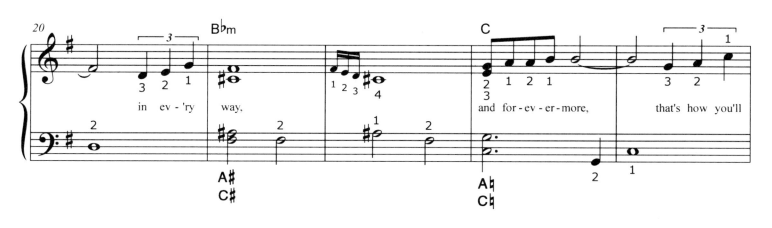

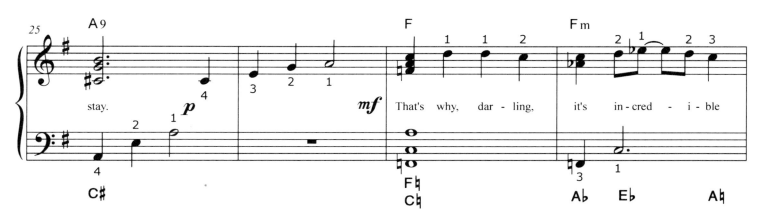

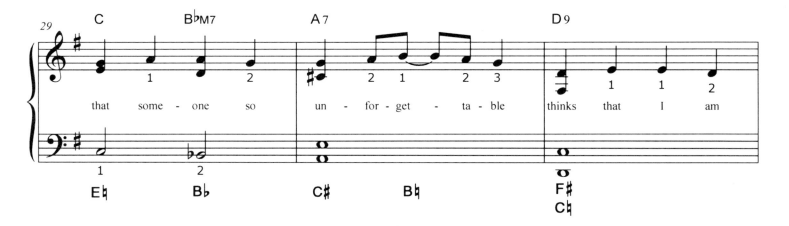

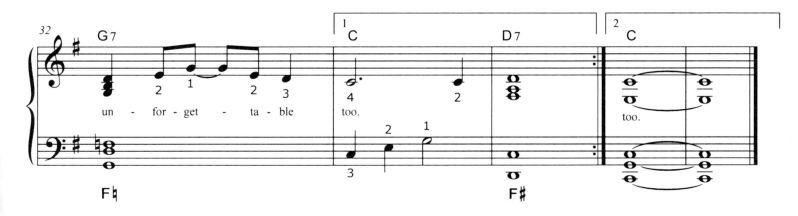

More Sheet Music Arrangements for Harp by Sylvia Woods

A Thousand Years
All of Me
All the Pretty Little Horses
America Medley
Disney-Pixar's Brave
Bring Him Home
Castle on a Cloud
A Charlie Brown Christmas
Two Christmas Medleys
Dead Poets Society
Everything
Fields of Gold
Fireflies
Flower Duet
Music from Disney's Frozen
Game of Thrones
Hallelujah

Happy
Happy Birthday to You
Harpers Are Not Bizarre
House at Pooh Corner
How Does a Moment Last Forever from Disney's Beauty and the Beast
In the Bleak Midwinter
Into the West
It's a Beautiful Day
La La Land selections
Disney-Pixar's Lava
Marry Me
Mary Did You Know?
My Heart Will Go On
Over the Rainbow
Photograph

River Flows in You
Safe & Sound
Say Something
Simple Gifts
Spiritual Medley
Stairway to Heaven
Star-Spangled Banner
Stay with Me
Disney's Tangled
That Night in Bethlehem
Unchained Melody
The Water is Wide
Mendelssohn's Wedding March
Winter Bells
Wondrous Love
Theme from Disney-Pixar's Up

Available from harp music retailers and www.harpcenter.com

Thanks
I'd like to thank the following harpists for their help: Paul Baker, Anne Roos, and Denise Grupp-Verbon.

© 2017 by Sylvia Woods
Woods Music & Books
Sylvia Woods Harp Center
PO Box 223434, Princeville HI 96722
www.harpcenter.com

U.S. $8.99

HL00254519

HAL•LEONARD® CORPORATION
7777 W. BLUEMOUND RD. P.O. BOX 13819
MILWAUKEE, WISCONSIN 53213

ISBN 978-0-936661-82-7

ONCE UPON A STRING FIDDLE METHOD

Volume 1

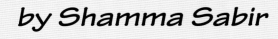

by Shamma Sabir

Art and Illustration by Sarah Parsons

Design and Layout by Charylu Roberts, O.Ruby Productions

Music Typeset by Shamma Sabir and Charylu Roberts

Photos by Brett and Kamran Beaulieu

ISBN 978-1-70510-773-7

EXCLUSIVELY DISTRIBUTED BY

HAL•LEONARD®

7777 W. BLUEMOUND RD. P.O. BOX 13819 MILWAUKEE, WI 53213

Dedication

To my husband, who encourages me to follow my passion for music education and all things music. To my parents who placed the first fiddle in my hands and encouraged me to grow in music. To all of the teachers along my path who have shared their knowledge and love of music with me. This includes the gentlest of teachers, Hedi Hein, who encouraged confidence in my abilities, and George Corneanu, the most compassionate and exacting of teachers, who supported me to hone my skills to a fine point. A heartfelt thank you to Sarah, Brett and Kamran Beaulieu for the beautiful technical photos in this book. A special thank you to two extraordinary fiddlers, my sister Roxanna Sabir and my sister at heart, Kim de Laforest, who edited this book and shared their insights and thoughts about the manuscript with me along the way.

About the Author

Shamma Sabir has been a passionate ambassador of Canadian fiddle music from the time she heard her first tune. A devoted teacher, Shamma has played and taught her way across much of the Canadian landscape and earned a Masters degree in Clinical Psychology using original research to further her understanding of the dance between music training and brain development. Shamma's first book, *Once Upon A String: Fiddle Fundamentals* can be found at music stores everywhere. *(shammasabir.ca)*

Credits

Kamran Beaulieu has been making music on his fiddle for five years and he continues to enjoy making music with his sibling and cousins who also play the fiddle. When not making music, Kamran enjoys Taekwondo and playing with his friends.

Brett Beaulieu finds inspiration in the people and the landscapes around him. Brett's photographic lens reflects a passion for children and families in particular, but also a love of the natural world. Brett can often be found out on the trails and waterscapes of the Fraser Valley, looking for the perfect shot. *(Instagram: Brett_Beaulieu)*

Sarah Parsons lives in West Kelowna, British Columbia. Sarah's painting style involves a love affair with acrylic and mixed media on wood. The beautiful swirling landscapes of the Okanagan Valley are a great inspiration for Sarah's paintings and drawings. Many of her paintings depict animal characters with a special fondness for pigs. *(sarahparsons.ca)*

Table of Contents

How To Use This Book

How To Use This Book

Welcome to **Volume 1** of the **Once Upon a String Fiddle Method.** This is the second book in the *Once Upon a String* series and builds upon important beginning theory and concepts presented in *Once Upon A String: Fiddle Fundamentals.* This book is intended for use as a step-by-step teaching guide for violin and fiddle teachers, and as a helpful resource for students and parents of students.

Warming Up: It is important to begin each practice session with stretches and exercises before proceeding to scales, easy warm-up pieces and finally, tunes. Section Two of this book, "Fiddle Warm-Ups," guides you through the process of getting your body warmed up to play. Many of these exercises have the added benefit of reinforcing great technique. *This is a key aspect of practice that is often overlooked by students.* Warming up in this way will build, reinforce and automate your technical skills, so the production of beautiful sound begins to feel effortless.

Practice Duration: If you are able to separate your practice into shorter segments, you will find that you progress much faster with intense concentration for a shorter amount of time. I recommend practicing for 10–15 minutes a few times a day. This is especially true if you are new to the fiddle and have a difficult time maintaining correct posture for longer periods of time. Try setting a timer for 10 minutes to start, and note at the end of the 10 minutes how your body feels and how strong your technique and concentration are. If you are just fine, try adding 5 minutes to your next practice. If you are struggling, reduce your next practice session by 5 minutes. If you are practicing consistently and mindfully, your skills will continue to grow!

Left and Right Hand Practice: The object of many of the exercises in this book is to separate left and right hand practice. Trying to tackle technical points on both sides simultaneously can feel overwhelming and defeating. When focusing on *left* hand technique points, do not worry about what your *right* arm may be doing, and vice versa. With careful practice, and as you develop automaticity on each side, you will notice that both arms work together to create great tone and intonation.

Exercises: I always tell my students that if you have a grass stain on a pair of pants, you can wash the pants over and over and that stain may fade, but it will never go away. In order to get rid of a stain you have to scrub that spot until the stain is gone, and *then* wash the pants. It is the same with practicing. If there is a section of a tune in which you make mistakes every time you get to that spot, practicing the whole tune over and over will not eliminate the mistake. Instead, you need to practice that spot in *isolation* until you are able to play it comfortably and with confidence, and then practice the whole tune. You will see that I have created short exercises for areas of each tune that prove to be especially challenging to students and for areas that introduce a new technical challenge. Be sure to give these exercises extra attention so that your tune doesn't have any grass stains!

Playing in Tune: In the beginning it will likely be challenging to play in tune. Don't worry! I have a few suggestions for you. My first recommendation is to make sure that your fiddle has tapes on the fingerboard for first, second and third finger placement. If your fiddle has these tapes already, check with your teacher to be sure that they are placed correctly, so that when you set your fingers down on the tapes they are in tune. If your fiddle did not come with finger tapes, ask your teacher to put them on for you, or take your fiddle to a music store where someone might be able to do this for you. My second suggestion is that you practice with a *tuner* so that you can check your intonation periodically or whenever you play certain notes. You will want to ask your teacher to show you how to do this as you progress. Finally, as you begin to develop a sense of what being in tune sounds like, you can also listen for extra resonant notes on the violin. These are notes that "ring" beautifully when you play them exactly in tune.

Find a Practice Buddy: The fiddle is an instrument that has traditionally been played at jam sessions and gatherings to add to the festivity of an event. You will find that if you can find a group to play with or someone to practice with from time to time, you will enjoy your practice sessions much more!

Listening is Learning: The more familiar a melody is, the easier it is to learn. It will be very helpful to listen to the tune(s) that you are learning ahead of time. When you are able to hum the tune, you will be in a place that makes learning it much easier. This is because the load on your working memory will be greatly reduced since you are now familiar with the song as a whole, and not as a series of unfamiliar notes that are harder to remember.

PRACTICE TIP

Whenever you see this symbol, I have given you a tip
that will help you master a certain aspect of your playing.
Pay attention to these sections as they will provide you with helpful
reminders that will help take your playing to the next level!

I CHOOSE A CHALLENGE

This symbol lets you know that if you have mastered the basic
technique and notes in a particular section, you can choose
to try something a little bit more difficult or go a little bit
farther with the concept. Go ahead—challenge yourself!

Fiddle Warm-Ups

Fiddle Warm-Ups

As you practice, you may notice that at times you are gripping the violin or bow too tightly. Practicing while tense can result in pain in your neck, back, shoulders and hands. Further, when your body does not have freedom of movement the fiddle is stopped from "singing" freely and it becomes very difficult to create the sound you would like to hear.

In *Fiddle Fundamentals* you may have noticed that right from the beginning we worked to develop healthy techniques that allowed us to hold the violin comfortably and to hold and move the bow freely. In this section I will show you some warm-up exercises for the body, the bow arm and the left hand. Several of these exercises are particularly good for helping to maintain a relaxed body posture. Other exercises will support the development of bow hold automaticity so that you are able to maintain a consistent bow hold when your bow arm is in motion. Warm-up exercises for the left hand will help get your fingers moving in a relaxed and organized way.

Warm-Ups for the Body

As you become more aware of your physical connection to the fiddle you may notice that you become increasingly tense throughout your practice. Noticing this is a great first step as it allows you to then stop, stretch your neck and shoulders, and release the tension. Try these simple stretches before you begin your practice, as needed throughout your practice, and again when you are finished.

The Fiddler's Prayer

This exercise, given its name by the great Canadian fiddler Gordon Stobbe, works to help you to stretch the muscles in your hands, wrists and forearms.

Start in a comfortable seated or standing position, then place your palms together and lower your hands until you feel a comfortable stretch. Hold your hands in this position for 20–30 seconds. Keeping your shoulders low and relaxed, be careful not to deepen the stretch too much or too quickly. To release the stretch simply bring your fingertips up slightly toward the ceiling and move your arms to either side. Make circles in the air with your hands to finish the stretch.

Neck Stretches

Due to the way we hold the fiddle *and* because of the way we hold tension in general, it's very important to allow the muscles of the neck to loosen and release this tension. These stretches can be an excellent addition to your practice routine.

Left-Right Tilt: Stand comfortably with your back straight, your shoulders relaxed, your head squarely over your shoulders and your weight distributed evenly over both legs. Tilt your head to the left so that your left ear moves toward your left shoulder. Stop when you feel a stretch and hold for 5–10 seconds. Remember to breathe deeply throughout your stretch. Release the stretch by bringing your head back to center. Repeat these steps for the right side. You can do several repetitions of this stretch on each side. If you are comfortable and wish to deepen the stretch, place finger-tips (left hand for left tilt and right hand for right tilt) on your head and press very gently. Children should not use their hand to deepen this stretch without adult supervision.

Side-to-Side: This stretch can be done in a comfortable seated or standing position, with your back straight, shoulders relaxed and your head squarely over your shoulders. Slowly turn your head to the left, noticing your range of movement and the sensation of stretch in your right neck and shoulder. Hold this stretch for 20–30 seconds while making sure that you are breathing deep breaths throughout. Slowly return your head to center. When you are ready, do the same on your right side. You can do several repetitions of this stretch as needed.

Shoulder Rolls

Because our arms are generally in a "lifted" position while we play the fiddle, our shoulders can often become overactivated, resulting in too much tension. It is important to remember to keep our shoulders low and relaxed when practicing. These shoulder rolls are a good way to release the extra tension that we often carry in our shoulders.

In a comfortable standing or seated position, with your back straight, shoulders low and relaxed and your head squarely over your shoulders, bring your shoulders straight up towards your ears. Slowly roll your shoulders forward, making big circles. After 5–10 shoulder rolls, repeat the same, but this time roll your shoulders backward.

Chest Stretch

Being in playing position can sometimes lead us to hunch our back and shoulders, shortening the big muscles in the upper chest. To stretch these muscles, stand with your feet a shoulder-width apart and with your knees slightly bent. With your abdominal muscles activated, roll your shoulders back and bring your elbows up to shoulder level, with your elbows at a 90-degree angle to your forearms. Your hands should be open with palms facing forward, so you look like a cactus. Slowly push your hands back, squeezing your shoulder blades together and opening up your chest. Hold this stretch for 20-30 seconds being sure to breathe deeply into the stretch. Repeat as needed.

I CHOOSE A CHALLENGE

These are some simple stretches that will allow you to bring awareness and looseness to your body as you get used to holding the fiddle and bow.
There are many, many more stretches that you can find online, and I encourage you to explore them when you are ready.

Warm-Ups for the Bow Arm

You may have noticed that you have a beautiful bow hold UNTIL you put the bow to the string and begin playing. After a few notes, your fingers rearrange themselves into an unrecognizable death grip. You don't notice this right away because your attention is on the left hand. Does this sound familiar? Don't worry, this happens to everyone in the beginning. It just means that you are still building automaticity with your bow hold, particularly when the bow is on the string and moving. Read on for the solution!

In *Fiddle Fundamentals* we started with two very important bow hold exercises to help you build strength, flexibility and automaticity in your bow hand: *Windshield Wipers* and *Pinky Push-Ups*. It will be important to continue to incorporate these exercises into your practice routine as you spend more time with your fiddle. You will notice that the more proficient you become with these exercises, the fewer finger placement corrections you need to make over several cycles of each exercise. Once you notice the development of flexible stability in your bow hold, you can begin to incorporate the following exercises, which will promote consistency in your bow hold *while the bow is in motion* AND *while your attention is completely focused on your bow hold*. This makes all the difference. You'll see!

Stir The Pot

This is an exercise that calls for some imagination—perfect for fiddle players! In a seated position and holding the bow so that the tip of the bow is pointed at the ceiling, imagine that there is a big cooking pot sitting on the floor between your legs. Using a counterclockwise stirring motion, imagine that you are stirring ingredients around the cooking pot. If you are a teacher or a parent of a younger student, try having students sit (on chairs) around one big cooking pot, contributing silly ingredients to seasonal soups (think Halloween soup, Christmas soup, and so on). As you stir, here are some points to keep in mind:

1. Keep your wrist relaxed; imagine a small amount of resistance in the "soup" that you are stirring, so that your wrist and hand are moving flexibly as you stir.

2. Ensure that your hold on the bow is loose and relaxed; the key to a great bow hold is a relaxed and flexible grip. This translates to producing sounds and rhythms on the fiddle that are connected, clear and lilting, as opposed to stilted and scratchy. This is why I am careful to refer to holding the bow as a bow *hold*, and not as a bow *grip*.

3. Notice if or when your bow hold moves out of alignment and correct it as necessary.

4. Close your eyes to experience what a correct bow hold *feels* like as you are moving the bow arm. Remember that once you are playing your fiddle, you really won't be able to watch your bow hold. It will be important to be familiar with the sensations associated with a correct bow hold.

The Rocket Ship

Using the same technique as you did in *Stir the Pot,* point the tip of the bow toward the ceiling. Slowly raise your arm so that your bow moves toward the ceiling like a rocket ship. Checking your bow hold as you go, bring your bow back down to the starting point. Keep points 2 to 4 in mind from the *Stir the Pot* exercise.

The Airplane

This exercise is similar to the *Rocket Ship* except that the bow is oriented horizontally to the ground, as it would be if you were playing your fiddle. With movement originating from your elbow rather than your shoulder, move your bow back and forth in front of you along a horizontal plane. Try to move your bow along an imagined straight line, so that your wrist gently flexes up and down to accommodate the movement of the bow on its path. You will notice that in contrast to the *Rocket Ship* exercise, there is more pressure on the pinky, as the pinky is now supporting the weight of the bow as gravity pulls on it. This will be a sensation similar to what it feels like to move your bow across the string, particularly as you near the frog and the rest of your bow hangs over the violin unsupported. This is why it's important to have a strong pinky, so that it doesn't collapse or lock while it balances the weight of the bow. Remember, a locked finger is the opposite of a relaxed and flexible finger, and will affect the fluidity of your playing. If you are having difficulty with your pinky, review the *Pinky Pushups* exercise in the *Fiddle Fundamentals* book in this series.

Write Your Name in the Air

This is a difficult exercise to do correctly—go slowly to start. With your right elbow bent and your right wrist and shoulders relaxed, point the tip of your bow in front and slightly to the left (it will want to point this way). Allowing your wrist and fingers to be relaxed and flexible, but without losing the correct hold on the bow, see if you can write your first name in the air. You will notice quite quickly whether your fingers are able to manage the small movements of the bow with strength and flexibility, or if they lock, grip the bow too hard, or slip out of place. Practice writing very slowly, a few letters at a time, until you can write your name with ease. Once you are able to do this, try writing your full name.

Circle Bows

Many of the tunes you'll be playing in this book require you to use a "circle bow" to move your bow from one down bow stroke to another down bow stroke. A circle bow allows you to move your bow back into a down bow position (⊓) for the beginning of the next phrase. I call this a "circle bow" because the right hand is making a small, counterclockwise circle as it carries a down bow off the string, continuing a counterclockwise circle upward into the air, and setting the bow carefully down onto the string again. Watch for the circle bow symbol throughout this book. It looks like this: ↺

Here are three important components of a good circle bow:

1. Make your circle small and tight so that as you set the bow back down on the string, you can do so quickly without allowing it to bounce or scratch.

2. Bring the bow to a full stop on the string before drawing it across the string again on a new down bow. This helps you control the onset of movement, the stability of the bow, and the sound you are making as you start the first note of the next phrase.

3. When you set the bow back down on the string make sure your bow is parallel to the bridge and on the Kreisler Highway. For more on this, refer back to *Fiddle Fundamentals.*

It's a good idea to incorporate circle bows into your exercises because a good circle bow is a test of your bow hold. In the beginning, as soon as you lift your bow from the string, your right pinky will want to collapse. This changes your bow hold as you start the next phrase. Circle bow exercises allow you to reinforce your strong and flexible bow hold, and help you to be attentive to the small movements that allow you to begin your next notes with great tone.

Ready for the exercises? Circle away!

Half Note Circle Bows

For each half note begin in the middle of the bow and play two counts toward the tip. Then, take your bow off of the string and place it back on the string in the middle for the next note.

BOW HOLD EXERCISE CHECKLIST

1. *Keep your right wrist relaxed.* Is your wrist moving flexibly as you move through the exercise?

2. *Ensure that your hold on the bow is loose and relaxed.* Can you see some movement in your fingers as you complete each exercise?

3. *Notice* when your bow hold moves out of alignment and correct it as necessary.

4. *Practice with your eyes closed.* What does it feel like to use a loose and flexible bow hold that balances strength and flexibility? Can you tell where your fingers are? Open your eyes and check, adjust if necessary, then close them again.

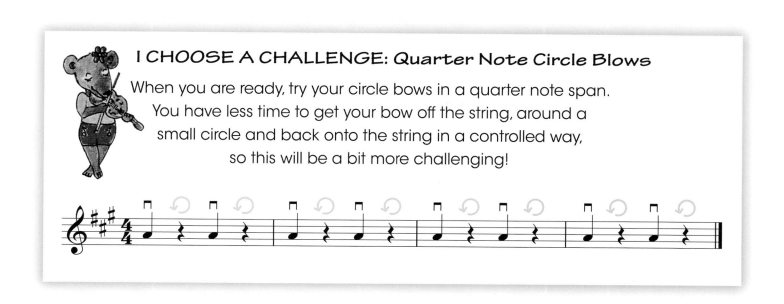
Warm-Up For The Left Hand

Once you've warmed up your body and your right arm it's a good idea to get the fingers of your left hand working smoothly and in an organized way. "Pingo Push" is one of the best warm-up exercises that I've come across in my travels. It supports fiddlers to focus on intonation and left-hand technique, as it introduces only one finger at a time for each 8-bar pattern.

Before you begin playing review your checklists from *Fiddle Fundamentals*. I recommend having them somewhere visible, such as on a wall or music stand.

Pingo Push
(Excerpt)

Andrea Hansen

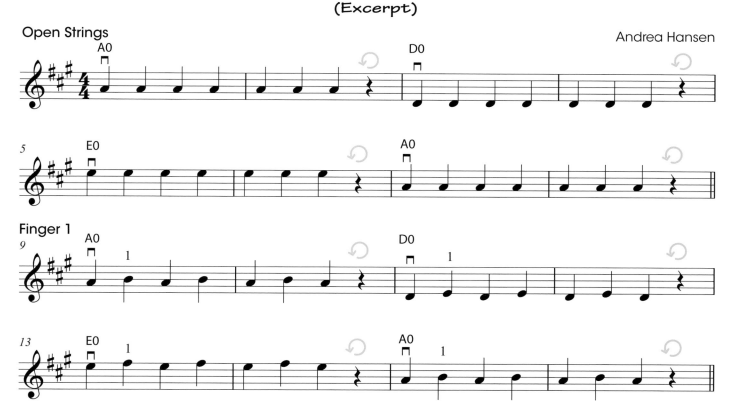

Finger 2

Finger 3

This is a shortened version of "Pingo Push," written by Andrea Hansen, a fiddler and composer who founded the not-for-profit organization Strings Across the Sky, providing violin and fiddle instruction to youth in the High Arctic, First Nations and Metis communities across Canada. Andrea is no longer with us, but her legacy lives on in the many, many fiddlers whose lives she touched with music, as well as in this tune. Published with permission of SISU Music.

BODY WARM-UPS CHECKLIST

1. Fiddler's Prayer
2. Neck Stretches
3. Shoulder Rolls
4. Chest Stretch

RIGHT AND LEFT HAND WARM-UPS CHECKLIST

1. Stir the Pot
2. The Rocket Ship
3. The Airplane
4. Write Your Name in the Air
5. Circle Bows
6. Pingo Push

Brief Review of Fundamentals 3

Brief Review of Fundamentals

Before we shift our attention to the A major scale, let's ensure that you are playing with great technique! Here are some review points from *Fiddle Fundamentals.*

1. Check your bow hold (all fingers are rounded, including the thumb). Depending on where you are in your fiddle journey and the size of your hands, your thumb may be either settled on the metal piece on the outside of the frog (often considered a "beginner" bow hold), or leaning against the "bump" of the frog (more traditional bow hold).

Beginner Bow hold

Traditional Bow hold

2. Make sure your violin is sitting comfortably between your chin and shoulder.

3. Many exercises in this book are played on open strings. When you are not using your left hand, keep the fingers curled loosely over the strings so that they are relaxed.

4. When using left hand fingers, make sure that you are putting your fingers on the string on the fingertips and that you have a straight left wrist.

5. When putting the bow to the string, see if you can keep it on the "Kreisler Highway." This spot is about two bow hair widths away from the bridge. This is the place on the strings where you will be able to create the loudest and clearest *tone* (or quality of sound). You will find that as your bow moves away from the bridge toward the fingerboard, the tone becomes fuzzier and softer. Go ahead and experiment to find this sweet spot on your fiddle!

6. The mind follows the eyes, so wherever you are looking is what you will be focused on as you practice. This lovely young man is focused on working with his bow to keep it parallel to the bridge and on the Kreisler Highway. Eventually, our goal will be to close our eyes and play with our senses of hearing and touch, and ultimately with our heart and soul fully engaged with the music we are creating.

PRACTICE TIP

Remember to keep your *Fiddle Fundamentals* practice checklists for Bow Hold, Violin Hold and Left Hand close by for easy reminders!

Once Upon A Major

A Major Scale Orientation

In *Fiddle Fundamentals* we learned about the A major scale in depth. It's a good idea to review the A major scale and the exercises covered in *Fiddle Fundamentals* before beginning this next section. Having a good grasp of the A major scale and arpeggio will set you in good stead for the next tunes in this section.

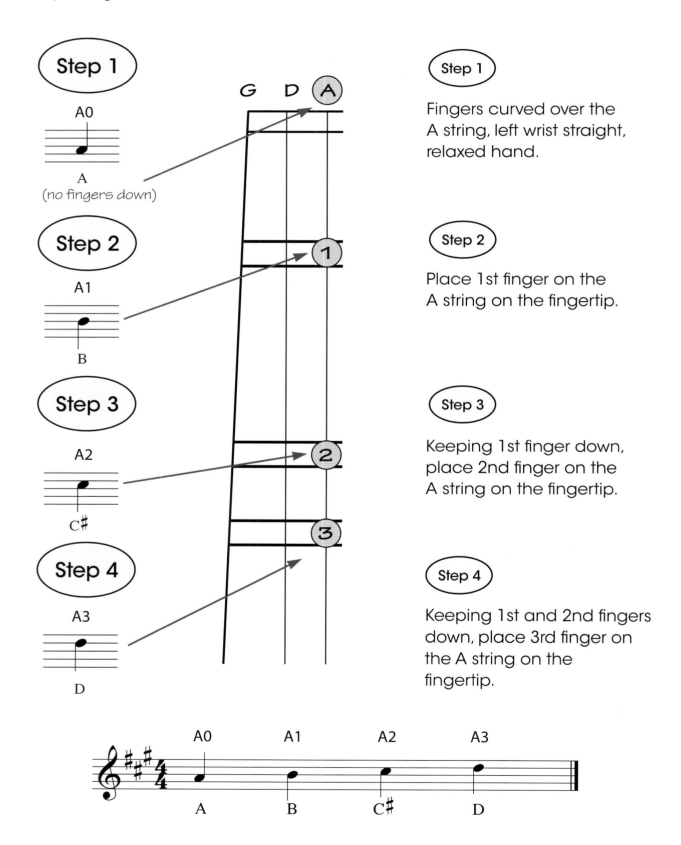

Step 1

A0

A
(no fingers down)

Step 2

A1

B

Step 3

A2

C#

Step 4

A3

D

Step 1

Fingers curved over the A string, left wrist straight, relaxed hand.

Step 2

Place 1st finger on the A string on the fingertip.

Step 3

Keeping 1st finger down, place 2nd finger on the A string on the fingertip.

Step 4

Keeping 1st and 2nd fingers down, place 3rd finger on the A string on the fingertip.

Step 5

Fingers curved over the
E string, left wrist straight,
relaxed hand.

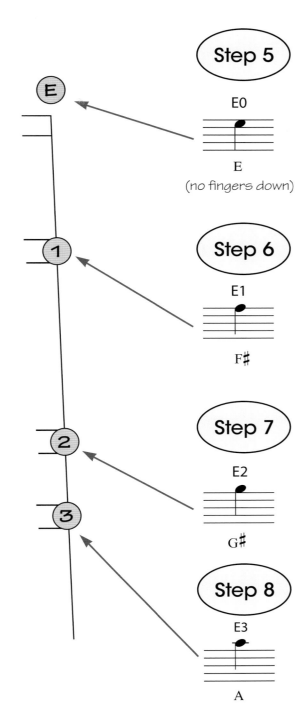

Step 5

E0

E

(no fingers down)

Step 6

Place 1st finger on the
E string on the fingertip.

Step 6

E1

F♯

Step 7

Keeping 1st finger down,
place 2nd finger on the
E string on the fingertip.

Step 7

E2

G♯

Step 8

Keeping 1st and 2nd fingers
down, place 3rd finger on the
E string on the fingertip.

Step 8

E3

A

I CHOOSE A CHALLENGE

Once you have familiarized yourself with the notes of the A major scale,
see if you can name each note after you bow or pluck it.
Don't forget to add the word "sharp" to the C♯, F♯ and G♯ notes.
For a bigger challenge, do the same but going back *down* the scale!

A Major Scale Review

The A major scale is an important building block on the way to becoming a proficient fiddler. Once you are comfortable with the notes, try incorporating one important aspect of technique each time you play the scale. Aspects of technique can include how you are standing, the bow hold, how the violin is sitting between your chin and shoulder, left hand posture, and playing in tune.

A Major Arpeggio: Skipping Around

The A major arpeggio is a type of scale that only uses the first, third and fifth notes of the A major scale. Try playing the arpeggio below. As you learn more fiddle tunes, you will find that scales and arpeggios make up parts of most tunes. This is why it's a good idea to make the A major scale and arpeggio a regular part of your warm-ups each time you practice.

New Concept: Ringing Notes (Playing in Tune)

For specific notes, the fiddle gives us feedback about whether we are playing in tune by producing a beautiful resonant sound that can still be heard after removing the bow from the string. This resonant sound often takes several seconds to fade away—much longer than your average note once the bow is off the string. I call these "ringing" notes. This happens because when played in tune, any note that has the same name as an open string (E, A, D or G) causes the open string to vibrate in response. As you get to know your fiddle, it's a good idea to learn where these notes are so that you may have the pleasure of listening for these special notes. If a smiling violin had a sound, these ringing notes would be it!

Exercise: Let It Ring

In the exercise below, be sure to lift your bow from the string after each note so you can listen for ringing notes. Be sure not to block the sympathetic string (the D string for the D note and the A string for the A note) by touching it with your finger. You can avoid blocking the ringing sounds by ensuring that your third finger is on the tip, and that your left wrist is straight.

Exercise: Target Practice

As your third finger learns to find its note target, you may not need to lift your bow off the string to hear the note ring inside the violin. Instead, you will hear a more subtle ringing sound. The exercise below allows you to train your ear to listen for it so that you know you are playing in tune without stopping the bow.

Exercise: Pingo Push Finger 3 Section

As you become more comfortable with finding ringing notes, see if you can play the following section of Pingo Push stopping on ringing notes D (A3), G (D3) and A (E3), to listen for ringing.

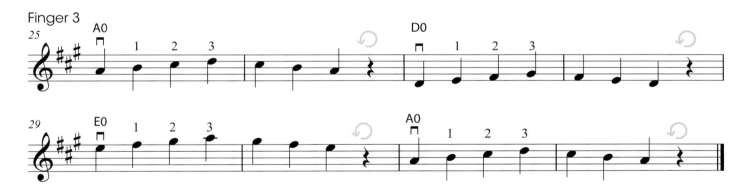

I CHOOSE A CHALLENGE

Once you have learned how to create ringing notes by placing your fingers on the string in tune, see if you are able create these lovely resonant notes as you play through the A major scale and arpeggio.

Memories of Paris

Traditional Folk Song (Waltz)

"Memories of Paris" is a *waltz*. Check out the time signature ($\frac{3}{4}$)—there are three quarter note beats in every bar! Have you noticed anything else that is interesting about this song yet? Here's a hint…look for a backwards A major scale!

Exercise: Keeping Fingers Down

When walking up a scale or a consecutive series of notes, it is necessary to keep fingers organized and in tune. You can do this by placing fingers on the fingerboard and leaving them down until they need to be moved again. This technique is indicated by the line underneath the 1st, 2nd and 3rd finger notes. In the first half of this exercise, after playing each 2nd finger note, lift fingers 1 and 2 off of the fingerboard to begin the next bar. This technique will be helpful when playing bars 9 to 11.

In the second half of the exercise, after playing each 3rd finger note, lift fingers 2 and 3 off of the fingerboard to begin the next bar. This technique will be helpful when playing bars 13 to 15 of "Memories of Paris."

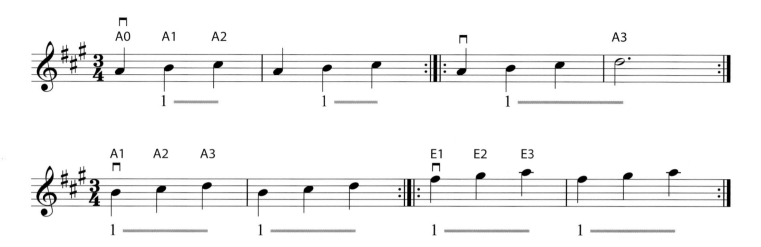

Exercise: Placing Three Fingers Down

For this exercise, place all three fingers down on the fingerboard for 3rd finger notes (*) so that fingers 2 and 1 are in place and ready to go as you move down the scale. Check for *intonation* (or whether or not you are playing in tune) by checking to see if your fingers are on the tapes. If you don't have tapes, try using a tuner. This technique will be helpful beginning in bar 17 of "Memories of Paris."

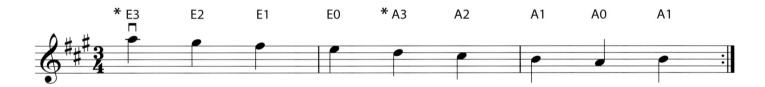

PRACTICE TIP

Once you are comfortable with this tune, see if you can listen for ringing notes on the A (E3) and D (A3) notes as you play. As you become more familiar with the unique sound your fiddle makes when you are playing these notes in tune, the easier finding them will become! *Listening* for ringing notes also encourages you to judge intonation by *listening* rather than by looking for finger placement on the tapes.

New Concept: The Top Half of the Bow

The purpose of bow division is to help understand how much bow is needed for each note so that we never run out of bow. This is often called *bow division*, because we mentally divide the bow into segments and use a specific amount of bow for longer or shorter notes.

In the beginning, the easiest part of the bow to use is the top half, or the part of the bow spanning the middle to a few inches shy of the tip. It would be helpful to have your teacher mark these places on your bow with some tape, as in the picture below, so that you are able to see the tapes as you play. For now, we are going to use the area of the bow seen in the pictures below.

Middle of the Bow

In the picture on the left, the bow is on the string in the middle of the bow. In this position, you will notice that the right elbow forms a 90-degree angle with the upper arm, and the bow is parallel to the bridge and at a 90-degree angle to the string. This is important for good tone production. It is important to note that you will want to mark the middle of the bow as being the place where your forearm and upper arm are at a 90-degree angle and your right wrist is flat. This may not be the physical middle of your bow. If you have shorter arms, it may be a bit closer to the frog, and if you have longer arms, it may be slightly closer to the tip.

The Tip End of the Bow

In the picture on the right, the bow is on the string at the tape closest to the tip. Note that the right elbow is now in an open position and the right wrist is extended slightly downward. The bow is still parallel to the bridge and at a 90-degree angle to the strings. It is important not to over extend the right wrist when playing at the tip of the bow. As such, the tape at the tip should be placed a few inches from the end of the bow where the wrist can sit in a comfortably extended position without stress or strain to the wrist and arm.

Exercise: Take Off and Landing

For this exercise, practice placing your bow on the string on each of the tapes as follows, repeating each three to five times: Middle-Tip-Middle/Tip-Middle/Tip. You won't be playing any notes, just lifting the bow off the string, placing it on the string on a specific tape, and lifting it up again. Once you have the feel of this exercise, try paying attention to the following:

1. The shape of the wrist should be flat when playing in the middle of the bow, and low, or valley shaped at the tip.

2. The bow hold should be stable but flexible. Be sure that your pinky finger is able to support the bow in a rounded shape, particularly when the bow is off the string.

3. The stick of the bow is tilted slightly away from you, but the hair sits flat on the string.

4. The bow is on the Kreisler Highway and parallel to the bridge.

Exercise: Middle to Tip of the Bow

For this exercise, begin in the middle of the bow. Using a down bow (⊓), move the bow slowly toward the tip. Then, using an up bow (⋁), move the bow slowly back to the middle. As you play, consider each of the following points:

1. The stick of the bow is tilted slightly away from you, so that the hair of the bow is flat on the string, and the stick leans slightly away from the bridge.

2. Your right wrist will be moving from a flat position (middle of the bow) to a comfortably extended position (tip) and back as you play.

3. Your bow moves along the Kreisler Highway, which is approximately two bow hair widths away from the bridge. The bow should remain parallel to the bridge as you play.

4. The fingers of your right hand move slightly and flexibly with the bow, but your bow hold remains intact as you play.

5. While the finger, wrist and elbow joints are moving along with the bow, the right shoulder does not move at all while you play.

Try cycling through these points as you play on the open A string, thinking about only one aspect of technique at a time. This is another great way to warm up each practice session!

Merrily We Roll Along

Traditional Folk Song

The time signature ($\frac{4}{4}$) indicates four quarter note beats in every bar.

Exercise: Bow Speed (Fast-Fast Slow)

The object of this exercise is to understand how quickly to move the bow for each note in order to stay comfortably in the top half of the bow. Try this exercise keeping your bow roughly in the areas suggested. When playing in the upper half of the bow, for now, don't go to the tip. Try to stay a few inches shy of the tip.

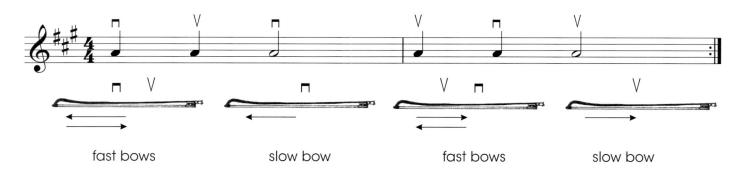

fast bows   slow bow   fast bows   slow bow

Exercise: Bow Speed/Changing Strings

Once you are comfortable with how to divide the bow, try this next exercise using the same bow division. In the first bar you will practice changing strings, and in the second bar, incorporate the left hand.

Boil Them Cabbages Down

Traditional Folk Song (Bluegrass Reel)

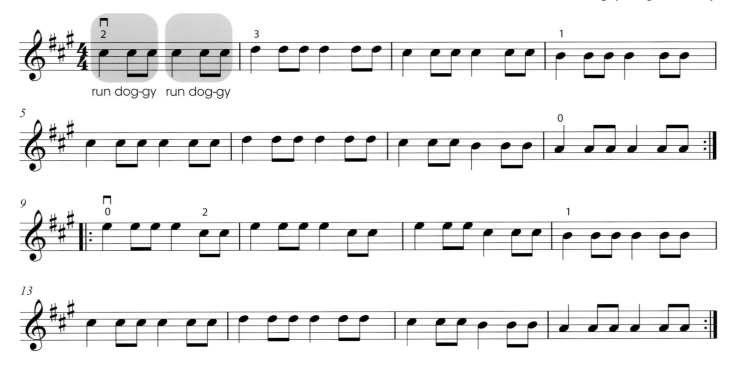

run dog-gy   run dog-gy

This tune uses the "run doggy" reel pattern that we talked about in the rhythms section of *Fiddle Fundamentals*. Just remember that there are two *run doggies* in each bar, and you will be playing this tune in no time!

Exercise: Long Short-Short

Let's focus on bow division. For this exercise we are going to continue to play in the top half of the bow. As you play the quarter note ("run"), use the entire space between the tapes on the top half of the bow. When you play the eighth notes ("dog-gy"), use only about half the amount of bow that you are using for quarter notes.

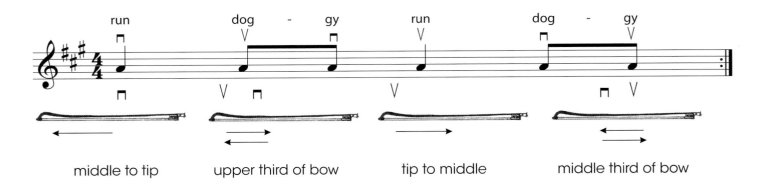

run   dog - gy   run   dog - gy

middle to tip   upper third of bow   tip to middle   middle third of bow

Exercise: String Changing/Keeping Finger 2 Down

This exercise has both a left and right hand focus. Focusing on the right hand will help you to change strings without making any squeaks or extra sounds. In order to do this, be sure to stop your bow between the E and A string notes. This will give you time to bring your right elbow up just slightly so your bow comes cleanly to the A string. As you become more comfortable with string-changing, you will gradually eliminate the extra time needed between notes. I have included quarter rests (𝄽) in the first two bars to give you one count to stop your bow and change strings.

The focus on the left hand will help you learn to keep your 2nd finger down on the A string while playing the open E string note, since you don't have a lot of time to get 2nd finger set up in this section. If you are playing on your finger tips and have a straight left wrist, you should be able to move cleanly and easily between the E and A string notes!

PRACTICE TIP

When you are playing "Boil Them Cabbages Down" at tempo, you won't need quite so much bow; using too much bow will only compromise your technique and slow you down. As such, once you understand this technique, feel free to try the same using slightly shorter bows, while still dividing your bow into quarter note and eighth note portions as shown in the Long Short–Short exercise on the previous page.

I CHOOSE A CHALLENGE

Once you are comfortable with the notes and technique in this tune, see if you can listen for ringing D (A3) notes as you play.

Lavender Blue

Traditional English Folk Song (Waltz)

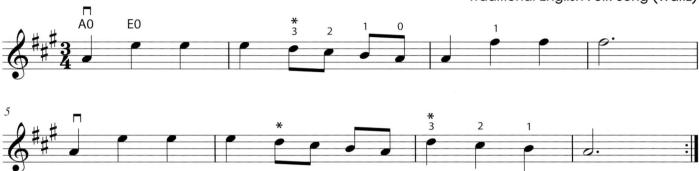

"Lavender Blue" is a *waltz* with three beats in every bar ($\frac{3}{4}$).

Exercise: String Changing From A to E

In "Boil Them Cabbages Down" we practiced moving the bow from the E string to the A string. This next exercise helps us to move in the opposite direction since the right hand and elbow move in a downward motion from the A to E string level. Remember, the key to clean string changing is making sure that you stop the bow between bow strokes.

Exercise: Finger Olympics

This exercise is similar to earlier exercises focusing on finger placement and intonation. Place all three fingers down on the A string to begin with (*). Take only one finger off the string at a time, until you arrive at open A. When you get to the second bar, place all three fingers down on the A string again. Repeat this until it feels easy! Remember to check to see if you are playing in tune by looking to see if your fingers are coming down on the tapes, or by using a tuner. You can also listen for a ringing D (A3) note!

Cripple Creek

Traditional Folk Song
(Bluegrass Tune)

Exercise: String Changing from E to A

This exercise will support you to spot practice the bow movement and fingering between strings in "Cripple Creek."

Exercise: Hello D String!

As you practice this next exercise, remember to bring your right elbow up a little higher to create strong, clear sound on the D string. If your bow touches the G string, your right elbow is too high, and if it touches the A string, it is too low.

Exercise: String Changing from A to D

This exercise is designed to help you change from the A to D string without making any squeaks or extra sounds. In order to do this, be sure to stop your bow between the A and D string notes. This will give you time to bring your right elbow up just slightly so your bow crosses cleanly to the D string. As you become more comfortable with string-changing, you will gradually eliminate the extra time needed between notes.

PRACTICE TIP

While you are playing the open A note, start curving your first finger over toward the D string so that it is on the string and ready when the bow starts moving.
Your first finger should be in place *before* you move the bow.

Exercise: Getting Finger 1 Ready Early

One of the goals of every fiddler is to be able to play faster and more fluidly. While a lot of that has to do with knowing the notes and the bowing, there are some other components involved as well, including how *relaxed* you are while playing, and how well you train your fingers to "think" ahead. This exercise focuses on supporting you to get your 1st finger ready while you are still playing the 3rd finger note, so that you can transition smoothly between notes and strings.

New Concept: The Whole Bow

Up until this point, you have been playing tunes and exercises in the top half of your bow. In this next section we're going to explore technique that will allow you to use your whole bow. The key to being able to use the entire bow lies in knowing how to move your right wrist.

The Frog End of the Bow

Let's have a look at the pictures below. In the picture on the left, notice that the right wrist is hill shaped when the bow is on the string and close to the frog. Once the bow reaches the middle (picture on the right), the wrist has become flat again. This movement of the wrist allows the bow to remain parallel to the bridge as it moves between the frog and the middle of the bow.

Exercise: Frog to Middle of the Bow

Try moving the bow between the frog and middle in the area marked in the picture above. Consider each of the following:

1. The stick of the bow is tilted slightly away from you, so that the hair of the bow is flat on the string, and the stick leans slightly away from the bridge.

2. Your right wrist will be moving from a raised position (frog) to a flat position (middle) and back as you play.

3. Your bow moves along the Kreisler Highway. The bow should remain parallel to the bridge as you play.

4. The fingers of your right hand move slightly and flexibly with the bow, and your bow hold remains intact as you play.

5. While the finger, wrist and elbow joints are moving along with the bow, the right shoulder moves only slightly as it accommodates the elbow movement toward the frog of the bow. In general, though, your right shoulder should remain low and relaxed.

Try cycling through these points as you play on the open A string, thinking about one aspect of technique at a time. As your technique becomes more automatic, try to incorporate as many points as possible. This is another great way to warm up each practice session!

Using the Whole Bow

The following exercises will support you to put this new technique into practice in order to begin using the whole bow.

Exercise: Take Off and Landing

For this exercise, practice placing your bow on the string on each of the tapes as follows, repeating each three to five times: Frog-Middle-Frog/Middle-Tip-Middle/Frog-Tip-Frog. You won't be playing any notes, just lifting the bow off the string, placing it on the string on a specific tape, and lifting it up again. Once you have the feel of this exercise, pay attention to the following:

1. The shape of your wrist should be high, or hill-shaped at the frog, flat in the middle of the bow, and low, or valley-shaped at the tip.

2. Your bow hold should be stable but flexible. Be sure that your pinky finger is able to support the bow in a rounded shape, particularly at the frog and when the bow is off the string.

3. The stick of the bow is tilted slightly away from you, but the hair is flat on the string.

4. The bow is on the Kreisler Highway and parallel to the bridge.

PRACTICE TIP

As you learn to use your whole bow you will rely a lot on your eyes to tell you how your bow and body are moving. However, it is important for your body to "just know" how to move correctly through muscle memory. When you are ready, spend some time with your eyes closed so you can feel your wrist and bow moving together.

Exercise: The Four Count Whole Bow

Now that we have explored how the right wrist moves when using the whole bow, let's focus on creating good tone. For this exercise you will need a metronome. There are many free versions that can be downloaded onto your computer or smart phone. Set your metronome to 60 beats per minute. This sets the pace of each beat. Beginning at the tape nearest the frog, traveling to the tape nearest the tip and back again, move the bow in a controlled way. Allow each bow stroke to take 4 beats to cover the distance between the frog and tip, and another 4 beats to move from the tip to the frog. As you become comfortable with counting, see if you can begin to incorporate the following points:

1. The frog end of the bow is heavier than the tip. To keep the tone and volume even across the bow, practice reducing pressure at the frog end, and adding slight pressure to the bow as you near the tip. You can gently add pressure by leaning your right hand into the index finger where it lays on the bow. As you near the frog again, take this pressure off of the bow.

2. Keep the fingers of your right hand relaxed and flexible on the bow. The more tightly you squeeze the bow, the shakier your bow will become. Think of the joints on your right hand as shock absorbers; maintaining a relaxed bow hold prevents a shaky sounding tone.

3. Make sure that your bow remains on the Kreisler Highway—this will give you strong, clear tone.

4. See if you can keep your bow parallel to the bridge at all times. When the bow moves off this track, tone can become squeaky or whispery. If you are struggling to see where your bow is, try standing in front of a mirror. Stand so that your violin runs parallel to the mirror, then lift your chin from the chin rest and turn your head toward the mirror to be able to see how your bow is sitting on the string.

Exercise: Changing Bow Speed

When we are playing different rhythmic patterns, we need to move the bow slower or faster depending on the length of note we are playing so that we don't run out of bow. For this exercise, we will practice changing the speed of the bow.

Keeping the metronome at 60 beats per minute, on a down bow, try using two full beats to move the bow from the frog to the middle (slower bow), and then one beat to move the bow from the frog to the tip (faster bow). When this begins to feel easy, on an up-bow, try using two beats to move the bow from the tip to the middle, and then one beat to move the bow from the middle to the frog. See if you can incorporate the technique points in the exercise above, focusing on only one point at a time.

Row, Row, Row Your Boat

Traditional Folk Song

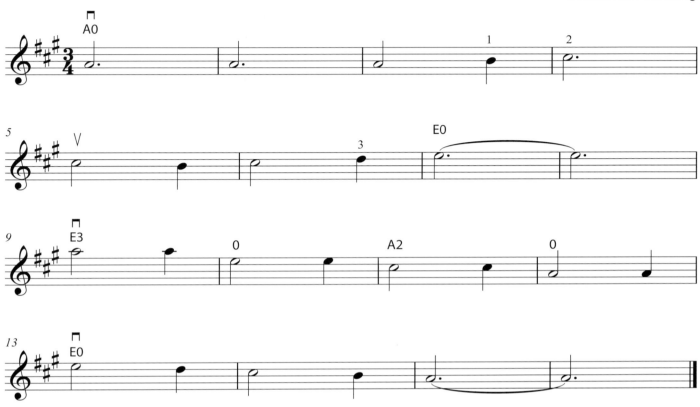

Have you spotted the backwards A major arpeggio in "Row, Row, Row Your Boat" yet? If you practice the arpeggio, this entire section of the song will be easy for you to play!

Exercise: Keeping Finger 1 Down

For this exercise, practice keeping finger 1 down for all four bars (indicated by the ———— symbol). This technique will help to keep your fingers organized and in tune. This exercise begins on an up-bow so that the bowing in this passage is consistent with the same passage in the song (bars 5 and 6).

Exercise: Long Up-Bows

This exercise supports you to plan ahead so that you don't run out of bow on the long up-bow in this song. First, try this exercise on the open A string so you can give your full attention to the bow arm. Once you have the bow technique, try adding in the left hand fingering in the section following.

Start in the *middle* of the bow, and while you are playing the first quarter-note, move your bow as close as you comfortably can toward the tip. When you are ready to begin the long (6 count) up-bow, you now have the whole stretch of bow available to you. Move your bow *slowly* over the six counts so you don't arrive at the frog too early. Remember to allow your right wrist to move to a hill shape as you near the frog.

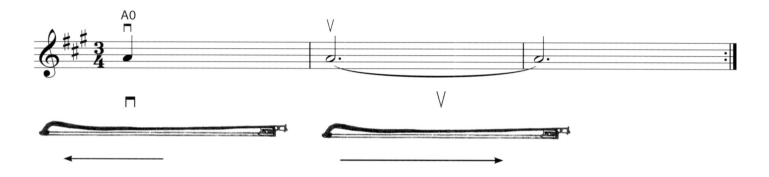

This next exercise uses the same bow division technique as the one above, but now you are including the fingers of your left hand in your attention. If you need to, take a small pause before changing to the E string to check your bow orientation.

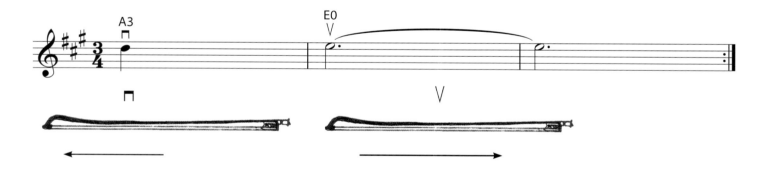

PRACTICE TIP

This tune has lots of slow bows and long notes. This is a great place to practice the Whole Bow techniques that you just learned. Remember to keep your body and particularly your right wrist nice and relaxed as you play.

Liza Jane

American Folk Song (Bluegrass Tune)

I CHOOSE A CHALLENGE: VARIATION

Once you finish the first four lines of this tune and you feel ready for a challenge, try the variation beginning at bar 17. Notice the run doggy rhythmic patterns that you are already familiar with!

You may have noticed that your fingers are beginning to need to move quickly in songs like "Liza Jane"—especially in the first two lines.

Remember to curve your fingers over the strings like an umbrella, so that your fingers are always close to the strings. That way, fingers 1 and 2 are always at the ready and when you are ready to play a little faster, your fingers won't let you down!

Exercise: Jumping Around!

A good habit to get into is to place finger 1 on the fingerboard when you are playing finger 2, and to place fingers 1 and 2 on the fingerboard when you are playing finger 3. This technique helps to support keeping your fingers organized and in tune as you play.

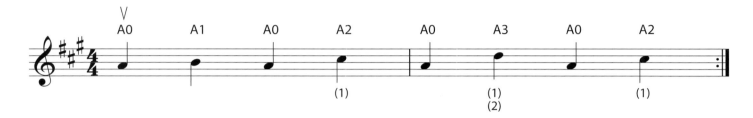

Exercise: Short Long Bow Division/Bow Speed on Open A

Some of the rhythms in "Liza Jane" are *syncopated*, meaning that the regular rhythm of the melody is interrupted. As you play these rhythms, it's possible to run out of bow if you are not thinking about bow division, since in this pattern, the down bow notes are shorter (quarter notes) than the up bow notes (half and whole notes). In this exercise, it's important to move the bow *slowly* over the half note, and *quickly* over the quarter note, so that you cover approximately half of the bow with each note.

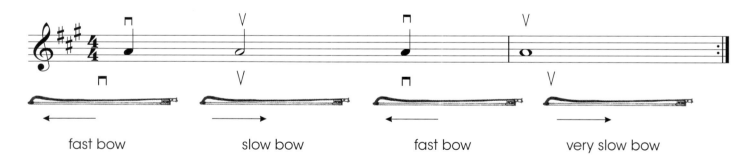

Exercise: Short Long Bow Division/Bow Speed With Left Hand

Once you understand how to control the speed of your bow when playing on the open A string, see if you can play the same rhythm again, this time with your left hand playing the notes of the song.

Shortnin' Bread

American Folk Song (Bluegrass Tune)

I CHOOSE A CHALLENGE: VARIATION

Once you finish the first four lines of this song and you feel
ready for a challenge, try the variation beginning at bar 17!

PRACTICE TIP

Bars 5 and 13 have the same "run doggy" rhythmic pattern that
we covered in the Long Short-Short exercise on page 29.

As you begin to increase your tempo, use slightly shorter bows while
still dividing your bow into quarter note and eighth note portions.

Rubber Dolly

English Folk Song

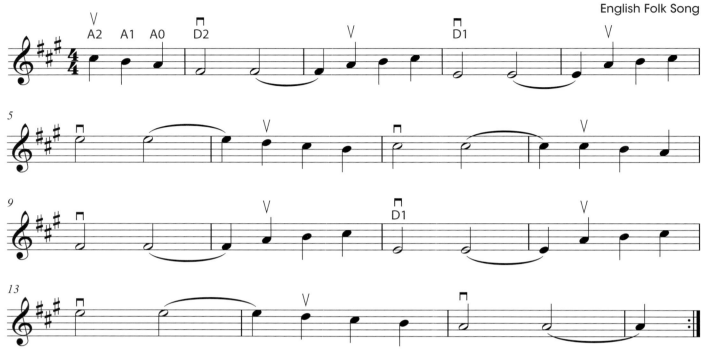

I CHOOSE A CHALLENGE: VARIATION

When you feel comfortable with the melody above, try this slightly busier variation. You can play this next section right after the more basic melody above.

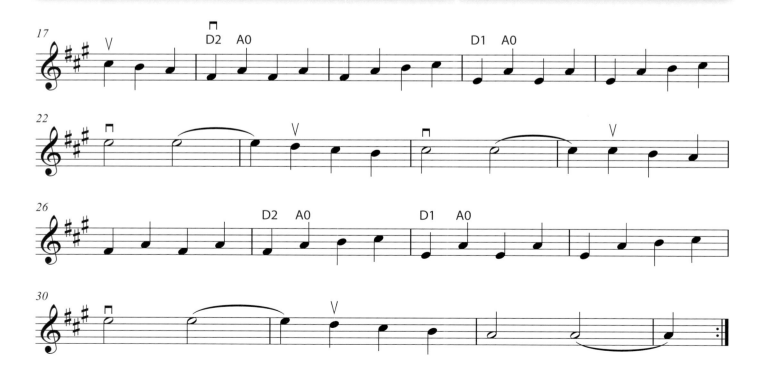

Understanding Tied Notes

A *tie* is a curved line connecting two notes of the same pitch together across a bar line. To count two notes that are tied together, just add up the counts of both notes. For example, in "Rubber Dolly," a half note (2 counts) is always tied to a quarter note (1 count), for a note that is held for 3 counts.

Exercise: Double Up-Bows

There are several places where a double up-bow is needed in "Rubber Dolly." Here are four exercises that will help you begin to get comfortable with double-up bows so that you don't get stuck at the frog.

- Exercise 1: Play four up-bow notes on the open D string, in the top half of your bow (a few inches from the tip to middle of the bow). Keeping your bow on the string, use small bows and practice bringing the bow to a full stop between each note.

- Exercise 2: On the tied note held for 3 counts, move your bow *slowly* to bring the bow to approximately the middle of the bow and no further, so you still have lots of room left for the final up-bow.

- Exercise 3: Now the exercise is beginning to resemble the same passage in the tune, as you will be starting on the same note. However, so that you can continue to focus on controlling the way you move your bow, the whole exercise stays on D2 (F#).

- Exercise 4: The final step! Change to an open A on the final note, using the technique you have been practicing in the first 3 exercises.

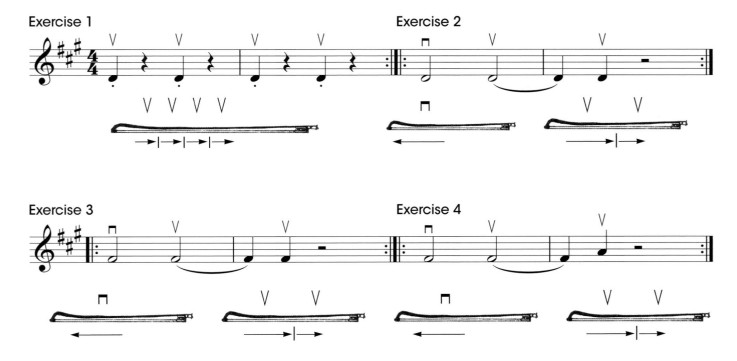

Chase Me Charlie

Traditional Scottish Jig

In a *jig* time signature ($\frac{6}{8}$) there are six eighth note beats in every bar.

Exercise: Double Up-Bow Spot Practice

The goal for this exercise is to ensure that you have enough room for two up-bows without getting stuck at the frog. Try this exercise using the bow division suggested below each note. Once you are comfortable with the bowing, try adding the fingering in bars 9 and 10.

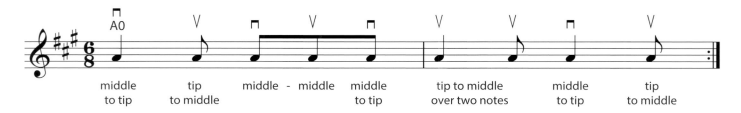

| middle to tip | tip to middle | middle - middle | middle to tip | tip to middle over two notes | middle to tip | tip to middle |

PRACTICE TIP

As you play through the double up-bows in the second part of this tune, see if you can keep your right wrist loose and flexible. You will know that you are nice and relaxed when you can see a small amount of movement in your wrist as you play over the double up-bow sections.

New Concept: Slurs

When you see a slur marking in your music, it means that you are to play the notes in the slur in one bow. In several of the next songs there are two notes included in each of the slurs, which means that you would play both of those notes in *one bow*.

Sometimes a slur begins on a *down* bow, and other times on an *up* bow. Try the exercises below to get acquainted with both. Try to stay in the top half of your bow (middle to close to the tip) as you play. Once this begins to feel comfortable, try playing in the bottom half of your bow. Begin a few inches from the frog, and bow to the middle and back.

Slur Exercise 1: The Slippery Bow

Slur Exercise 2: Slipping Up the A Major Scale

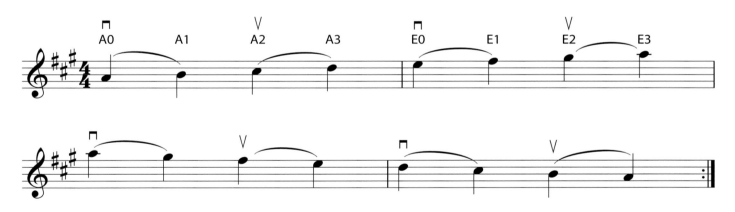

Slur Exercise 3: Circles and Slurs

For the exercise above, try preparing your bow early by placing it on the string in the middle for each down bow slur. For a clean sound, be sure that the bow is settled on the string and not in motion before beginning each slur. Once this begins to feel comfortable try playing in the bottom half of your bow.

Oh, Susannah!

American Folk Song (Bluegrass Tune)

Exercise: Counting a Pickup Measure

In fiddle music it is not uncommon to find that the first measure of music is not a full measure. Instead, we sometimes see a shortened first measure called a *pickup* measure. You will notice that in tunes with pickup measures, the last note (in this case, a dotted half-note) and the pickup notes (two eight-notes) add together to make a full measure (4 counts). For this exercise give your full attention to counting using the counts provided. You can count them out loud or to yourself, and imagine playing the notes over the appropriate beats, count while you clap the notes, or even ask someone else to count for you as you imagine or clap your way through the first two measures.

Exercise: Dotted Rhythms

A *dotted rhythm* is one in which a longer note is followed by a shorter note. The dot adds half of the time value of the note that it is attached to. In this exercise you are learning to count a dotted quarter note. Since a quarter note is one beat (counted as 1 +), adding a half a beat means it is now counted as 1 + 2. In this exercise the dotted quarter note falls on beats 3 + 4. Once you have played the rhythm through on the A string a few times, try adding in the left hand as shown in the next two bars.

1 + 2 + 3 + 4 +   1 + 2 + 3 + 4 +   1 + 2 + 3 + 4 +   1 + 2 + 3 + 4 +

PRACTICE TIP: FOCUS ON LESS

Here is a good example demonstrating how you might isolate key parts of this exercise so that you can really focus on one concept at a time before incorporating everything together. Try each step in sequence.

1. Counting only. You've already done this in the exercise on the previous page, but it's good to see it as a building block in a process that supports you to play any new or tricky passage.

2. Once you understand when to begin your first note, it's time to bring in the bow arm. Try substituting most of the notes as written for open strings. For example, you could play the first full measure on open A. This way you can really just focus on the pickup notes, and getting into the first full bar.

3. Then, play the pickup notes as written and the rest of the notes as the open string they are on (in this case, the A and E strings).

4. Finally, when you are ready, add in the left hand by playing the notes as written.

Exercise 1: Counting

1 + 2 + 3 + 4 +   1 + 2 + 3 + 4 +

Exercise 2: Open Strings

Exercise 3: Changing Strings

Exercise 4: Adding in the Left Hand

WHAT IS REVIEW?

This tune brings together many of the concepts that you've been learning so far in this book. Some concepts may still feel new and require a lot of concentration from you to be able to play correctly. Others may be starting to feel so comfortable that you may have been using these techniques without even realizing it.

As we learn, it's important to remember that the process of learning is not just that of acquiring new information, but also going back and relearning, reviewing and refining information you've already taken in. If you've forgotten some points, don't worry about it! Going back to see what you may have missed or forgotten is as important as learning new information. That's why *review* is a foundational component of learning.

While we have a look at all of the techniques that this tune brings together, I am also going to include the page numbers that you can find an explanation of the technique on so that you can go back and review if you need to. Let's start with the earliest techniques or concepts that you learned, and end with the most recent. As you look at each item, ask yourself where in "Oh, Susannah!" you might be using that particular technique:

- *Circle Bows* (Page 12)

- *Ringing Notes* (Page 22)

- *Keeping Fingers Down* (Page 24)

- *Placing Three Fingers Down* (Page 25)

- *Playing in the Top Half of the Bow/Using the Whole Bow* (Page 26/34)

- *String Changing* (Page 28/31/32)

- *Double Up-Bows* (Page 43)

- *Slurs* (Page 45)

- *Dotted Rhythms* (Page 46)

- *Counting a Pickup Measure* (Page 46)

Are you surprised at how much you have learned already? Congratulations! You are well on your way on your fiddling journey.

Cajun Two-Step

Composer Unknown
(Arranged by Shamma Sabir)

The Stool of Repentance

Traditional Scottish Jig

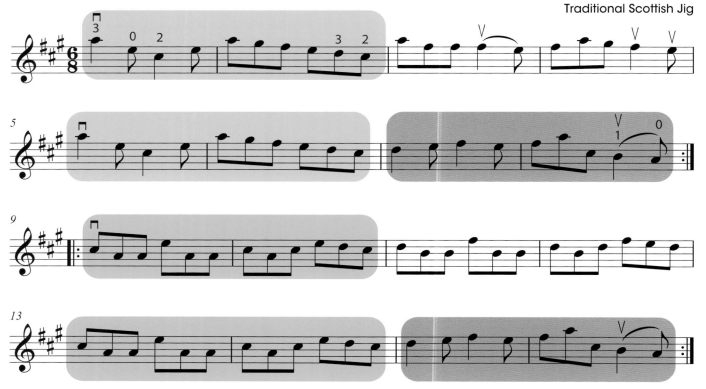

PRACTICE TIP: LOOK FOR REPEATED PATTERNS

As you play through this melody, notice that there are three sections that make more than one appearance in this lovely tune. This is very common in many styles of fiddle music and recognizing that you are already familiar with sections of the tune will cut down on your learning time. For example, in this tune, bars 1 and 2 are reused for bars 5 and 6, bars 7 and 8 are recycled again as bars 15 and 16, and bars 9 and 10 are used again as bars 13 and 14.

Exercise: Leaving First Finger Down (Bars 11 and 12)

Here is another opportunity to practice leaving your first finger in place. This allows you to play without tangling your fingers up! For this exercise, practice placing first finger on the fingertip evenly over both the A and E strings where you see finger 1 notated below. Remember to keep your left wrist straight and to keep your left hand relaxed as you practice.

Ger the Rigger

Traditional Irish Polka

Exercise: Triplet Rhythm

In bars 2 and 6 of "Ger the Rigger" there is a triplet rhythm, meaning that we are going to play three notes in the space of two. In order to accomplish this, each note gets slightly less time than you would normally give an eighth note. For the first exercise, try clapping the notes as you voice the rhythm. Then, play the rhythm on open A. Once you feel comfortable with this, try the next exercise slowly, playing the notes and the rhythm together.

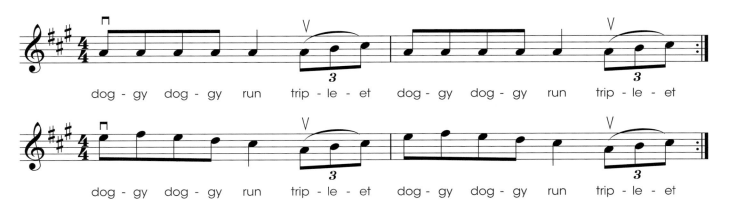

PRACTICE TIP

Can you spot the repeated patterns in this tune?

51

Refining Your Practice Routine

Congratulations! You are well on your way to playing the fiddle skillfully! If you have not done so already, please take a moment to give yourself a HUGE hug and a pat on the back. Now is a good time to take a glance backward so we can see all of the learning you have done to this point and put it to practical use by building it into your practice routine. To help you with this, I have created a practice chart for you here, with lots of room for you to choose what you would like to do each practice session.

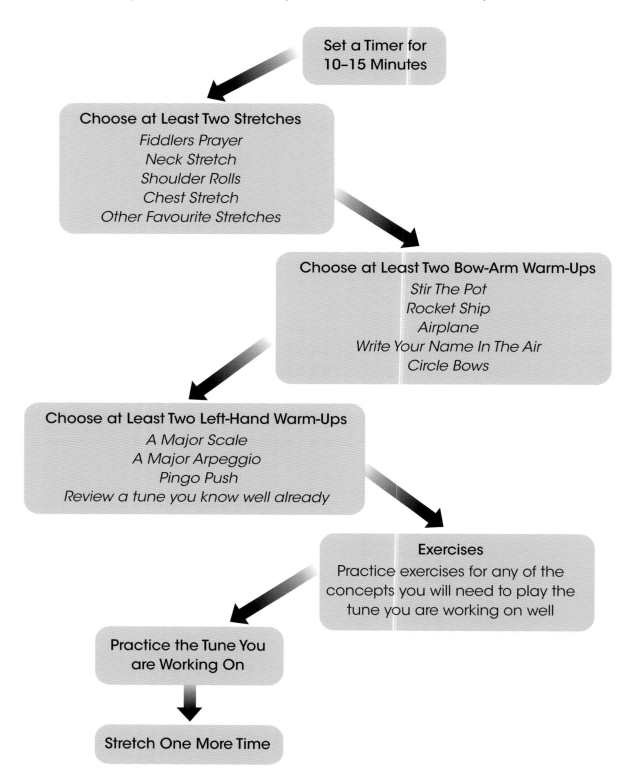

Set a Timer for 10–15 Minutes

Choose at Least Two Stretches
Fiddlers Prayer
Neck Stretch
Shoulder Rolls
Chest Stretch
Other Favourite Stretches

Choose at Least Two Bow-Arm Warm-Ups
Stir The Pot
Rocket Ship
Airplane
Write Your Name In The Air
Circle Bows

Choose at Least Two Left-Hand Warm-Ups
A Major Scale
A Major Arpeggio
Pingo Push
Review a tune you know well already

Exercises
Practice exercises for any of the concepts you will need to play the tune you are working on well

Practice the Tune You are Working On

Stretch One More Time

Once Upon 5 D Major

D Major Scale Orientation

In *Fiddle Fundamentals* we learned about the D major scale in depth. It's a good idea to review the D major scale and the exercises covered in *Fiddle Fundamentals* before beginning this next section. Having a good grasp of the D major scale and arpeggio will set you in good stead for the tunes in this section.

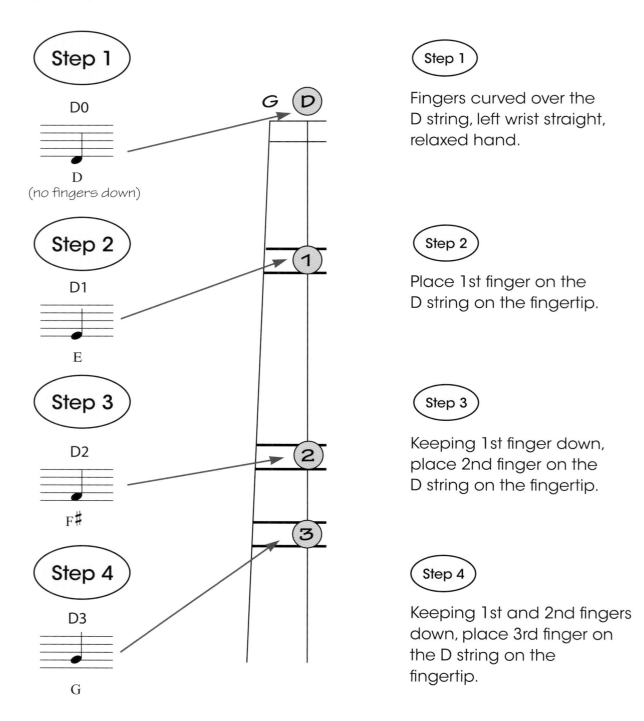

Step 1

D0

D
(no fingers down)

Step 1

Fingers curved over the D string, left wrist straight, relaxed hand.

Step 2

D1

E

Step 2

Place 1st finger on the D string on the fingertip.

Step 3

D2

F♯

Step 3

Keeping 1st finger down, place 2nd finger on the D string on the fingertip.

Step 4

D3

G

Step 4

Keeping 1st and 2nd fingers down, place 3rd finger on the D string on the fingertip.

Fingers curved over the
A string, left wrist straight,
relaxed hand.

Place 1st finger on the
A string on the fingertip.

Keeping 1st finger down,
place 2nd finger on the
A string on the fingertip.

Keeping 1st and 2nd fingers
down, place 3rd finger on the
A string on the fingertip.

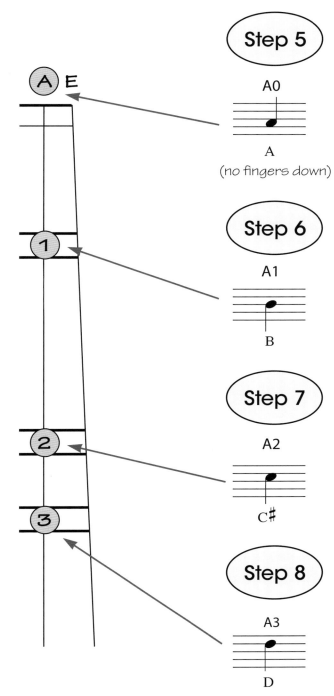

Step 5

A0

A

(no fingers down)

Step 6

A1

B

Step 7

A2

C#

Step 8

A3

D

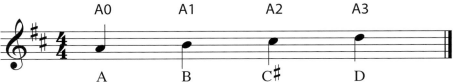

A0   A1   A2   A3

A   B   C#   D

I CHOOSE A CHALLENGE

Once you have familiarized yourself with the notes of the D major scale,
see if you can name each note after you bow it. Don't forget to add
the word "sharp" to the F♯ and C♯ notes.
For a bigger challenge, do the same but going back *down* the scale!

D Major Scale Review

The key of D major is a favourite for fiddle players, and there are hundreds of tunes written in this key. Learning the D major scale and arpeggio really well is your first step to being able to play many of these tunes!

Once you understand the notes, see if you can incorporate some of the important technique points that we talked about in *Fiddle Fundamentals* and earlier in this book, including:

- A great bow hold with a relaxed right hand;
- Your violin comfortably supported between your chin and shoulder;
- Good posture with relaxed joints;
- A left hand setup that allows your fingers to set down on the string on the tips.

If you think you may have forgotten any of these points of technique, go ahead and review! Remember that review is an important part of the learning process.

D Major Arpeggio: Skipping Around

Like the A major arpeggio, the D major arpeggio is a type of scale that only uses the first, third and fifth notes of the scale.

As you play through the D major scale and arpeggio, listen for ringing notes on the E (D1), G (D3) and D (A3) notes of the scale, and the D (A3) note of the arpeggio.

Exercise: Target Practice on the D String

Playing in tune is easier when we are able to slow down and focus on fewer things. This next exercise is an opportunity to focus on 1st and 3rd finger placement, listening for ringing notes.

Exercise: Finger Twisters

Between the D major and A major scales, we now know all of the notes from the D string to the E string on the fiddle. These next exercises will support you to get comfortable with moving your fingers quickly over all three strings.

The Left Hand: When you begin these next exercises focus on fingering and left hand technique. Begin by getting comfortable with the finger patterns. You might notice that as you become comfortable with the fingering and try to increase your tempo, your left hand begins to squeeze the neck of the violin. This will actually slow you down and cause difficulty with left hand technique. Instead, you can train your left hand to stay relaxed by focusing on a relaxed hand and thumb and a lightness in your fingers as they touch the string and pop off again.

The Right Arm: After you have played this exercise focusing on your left hand, shift your focus to the right hand. You will notice that there is quite a bit of string changing that happens in this exercise. Try to make your bow movements between strings small and economical so that you are able to play these exercises with ease over time. As with your left hand, remember to keep your right arm loose and relaxed as you play.

Putting it All Together: After focusing individually on right and left sides, see if you can play these exercises slowly with everything you have just practiced in mind. *It is a lot to remember, so above all, keep both hands and arms relaxed, and the rest will follow.* The more you develop automaticity with each technique point (or the less you have to think about each individual component), the easier putting it all together will become!

Finger Twister in 4/4

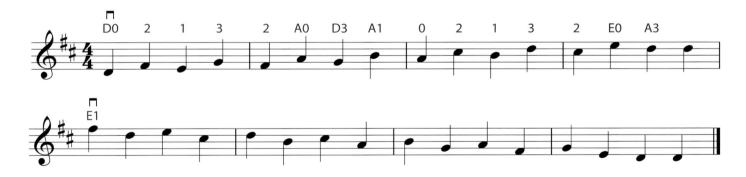

Finger Twister in 6/8

New Concept:
Low Second Finger on the E-String

In the key of D major, there are only two sharps—F♯ and C♯. Since there is no G♯ like there is in the A major scale, when you play second finger on the E string (the G note), you will place that finger lower, close to first finger instead of close to third finger. This is a new note for you, and it is called G natural (G♮).

Exercise: Target Practice for Lowered Second Finger

In the exercise below, be sure to place second finger low, close to the first finger, placing both fingers down at the same time. In this way first finger will act as an intonation guide for second finger. You will need to know where to find this note for the next songs in this book.

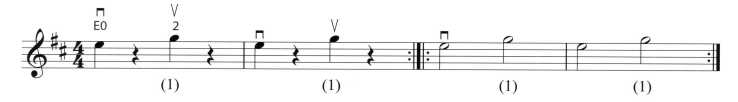

Exercise: Lowered Second Finger on the E String

Be sure to keep your left hand loose and relaxed in order to place third finger properly in tune. Both the G (E2) and A (E3) notes will ring when played in tune, so as you play through this exercise, listen for these ringing notes to guide your intonation.

Exercise: Tone and Intonation in D Major

This exercise is filled with notes that will ring beautifully when you play them in tune. Can you find all of the ringing notes? There are seven of them! As you play, use long strong bows, keeping your bow on the Kreisler Highway.

Exercise: Placing Second Finger Quickly

This exercise supports finger organization—keeping fingers down when they don't need to move—so that you can move fluidly up and down the fingerboard. The key to playing this exercise is to keep both your left hand and your bow arm loose and relaxed. Begin slowly and build your tempo up over time. You will know that you are ready to try this exercise a wee bit faster when you are able to stay relaxed at the tempo you are at. Use a metronome to be sure that you increase your speed in controlled amounts: one or two beats per minute at most.

PRACTICE TIP

As you become familiar with the fingering in this exercise and the Finger Twister exercises presented previously, keep in mind the following tips:

- Warm up with stretches;

- Do a body scan to ensure there are no points of tension anywhere in your body;

- Use a metronome to be sure that you increase your speed in controlled amounts: one or two beats per minute at most.

I'se the B'ye

Newfoundland Folk Song (Canadian Jig)

Exercise: Long Short Bow Division

"I'se the B'ye" uses a rhythmic pattern that is very typical for jigs. This pattern gives the jig its bouncy, lilting feel, and it can be more difficult to play than you might think! The reason for this is that the long notes, or quarter notes, fall on a down bow, and the short notes, or eighth notes, fall on an up bow. Typically, it takes more bow to play a longer note, so after repeating this pattern a few times, we can easily get stuck at the tip of the bow.

In this exercise, try to use the same amount of bow for both quarter notes and eighth notes. To do this, try moving the bow more slowly for quarter notes, keeping the bow between the middle and a few inches from the tip. For the final two notes use bigger, faster bows. As you become more familiar with the tune and your tempo increases, you will not need to use big bows. Until then, go ahead and use a bit more bow and play slowly.

Bow Speed: slow   fast   slow   fast   slow   fast   slow   fast   slow   fast   slow   fast   fast   fast

Old Joe Clark

American Folk Song (Reel)

The introduction in this tune requires you to play both the A and E strings for the four "run doggy" bow patterns. When you are playing on two strings at the same time, remember that you don't need to press any harder to play on two strings than you do to play on one string. You just want to keep the bow firmly and evenly over both strings, keeping your body and particularly your right wrist relaxed.

Technically, this tune is in the key of A major, but I have included it in this section because it follows a D major finger pattern due to the G♮ notes. Even though there is a G♯ in the key signature, the natural G is denoted by a natural sign (♮) in each bar in which a G note appears. When a note appears in music that is not a part of the key signature, it is called an *accidental*. As such, in this tune you will be playing a G♮ accidental.

New Concept: Tone Development

There is really nothing more beautiful than pulling gorgeous, rich sounds from the strings of a violin. Through this book we have worked on technique underlying good tone production. Here we will review that technique and introduce a few more technique points that will support the development of tone quality.

Review:

1. Posture. Remember that good posture is the foundation from which all other technique stems. It is important to be relaxed so that music can flow unimpeded from your mind, through your body, and again through your instrument.

2. Release Tension. As you are playing, scan your body for any points of tension. Tension has an immediate negative effect upon tone. If you are noticing areas of tension, stop and stretch immediately. If you notice that your tone is poor, do a quick body scan to find and release tension and bring looseness back into your body.

3. Kreisler Highway. Where the bow makes contact with the string will determine the sound you create. We have talked about the Kreisler Highway as being approximately two bow hair widths away from the bridge. Try experimenting in front of a mirror so you are able to see where your bow sits on the string, and what kind of sound it is making.

New Technique Points:

4. Pulling or Tugging the Bow. How the bow moves across the string is very important. Try to think about *pulling* the bow across the string and gently tugging sound from the fiddle, instead of pressing the bow into the string. Pulling the bow across the string creates open, rich sound, while pressing the bow into the string creates sound that is compressed and strained.

5. Listening and Feeling. As we learn to play the fiddle, we use our eyes perhaps more than our ears to see where we are placing our fingers on the strings, where our bow contacts the string, and to read the music. However, as you continue, keep in mind that *listening* and *feeling* will become more important than seeing. To start down this path, practice listening intensely to tone and intonation as you play scales and simple exercises, while also paying attention to how your body feels as you play.

Scales and simple exercises are perfect for developing clear, rich, controlled tone. Try playing through the A major and D major scales and review simple exercises and tunes that you know well in order to focus on tone development.

Planxty Hewlett

Turlough O'Carolan (Irish Waltz)

To play the first and second endings in "Planxty Hewlett," play as written to bar 8, then repeat, skipping bar 8 and playing bar 9. See page 64 for more on first and second endings.

Exercise: Hello G String!

To reach the G string with the bow, bring your right elbow up *slightly* from the D string level so that your bow is firmly on the G string and is no longer touching the D string. Remembering that we want our movements to be economical and small, the bow only needs to just lift off the D string to sit on the G string, it does not need to lift high off of the D string, as we will want to bring it back to the D string quickly for the next note!

River John Sunset

Florence Killen (Canadian Waltz)

New Concept: First and Second Endings

"River John Sunset Waltz" is another tune with first and second endings. The role of these endings is to optimize the amount of space on the page of a musical score, so large parts of the melody are not written out again when a repeat will do. To read through "River John Sunset" correctly, play the repeat as you normally would. However, on the second time through when you get to the end of bar 4, skip over the first ending—bars 5 through 8—and play the second ending beginning at bar 9. The same thing happens in the next section—after playing through the first ending, repeat, skipping over the first ending and playing through the second ending to the end. It's a bit like reading a musical map!

Exercise: Counting the Pickup Measure

For this exercise, try giving your full attention to counting using the counts provided. Count out loud or to yourself while imagining playing the notes over the appropriate beats. You can also count while you clap the notes or ask someone else to count for you as you imagine or clap your way through the two measures. Once you are able to anticipate when the first note is played, go ahead and play the pickup.

Exercise: Bow Division and Tone Development

Using the bow division suggested below, see if you can play the notes in each exercise thinking about tone. Be sure to pay attention to your posture before beginning. How much do you need to *pull* on the bow to *tug* deep, rich sound from the strings? Remember to bring your right wrist up into a hill shape as you move past the middle point of the bow toward the frog.

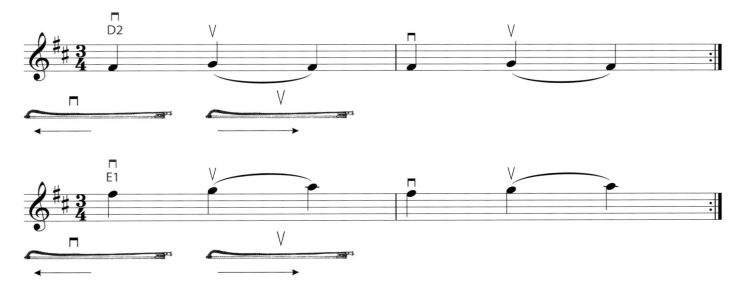

Exercise: Playing a Double Stop

A *double stop* means to play two notes on adjacent strings at the same time. In the exercise below, the first two bars allow you to play the double stopped notes individually so that you can hear if the individual notes (particularly the F♯ or D2 note) are in tune before playing them together. The next two bars support you to move smoothly into the double stop.

Andy Dejarlis Jig

Andy Dejarlis (Métis Jig)

Exercise: Seesaw

Up until this point, we have focused on using either the top half of the bow or the whole bow. When changing strings rapidly, however, as in the "Andy Dejarlis Jig," it is important to be economical with right arm movement in order to play in a way that is both at tempo and relaxed. The best place to play a jig with rapid string changing is the middle third of the bow. To illustrate this, try the following exercise at three different places on the bow: the top third, the middle third, and the bottom third.

You will notice that you need to move your right arm in a wide arc to change strings when you play in the top third of the bow, making bow and arm movements unwieldy. When playing in the bottom third, near the frog, the bow arm is cramped and there is too much weight on the bow to play quickly, since this is the heavier end of the bow.

When playing in the middle third of the bow there is a much smaller arc created when changing strings, leading to smoother bow movements. As you practice in the middle third of the bow, keep the right wrist loose and flexible.

Ingonish Jig

Traditional (Irish Jig)

Exercise: Big Bow Before a Slur

In this exercise, use the *accented* (>) or *emphasized* E note to move the bow close to the tip end of the bow, and allow the three-note slur to bring the bow back to the middle. Now you are set up in the middle of the bow for the next notes of the tune.

Exercise: Accent in the Second Half of a Slur

Though the notes are different, the bowing and bow division for each of the three bars of this exercise are the same. Play the first two notes in the middle of the bow, using about the same amount of bow for each. Use the middle to close to the tip of the bow for the next two slurred notes, using more bow for the accented note. The final up bow slur should take the bow from the tip back to the middle, with approximately the same amount of bow for each note.

Londonderry Hornpipe

Traditional (Irish Hornpipe)

The time signature for "Londonderry Hornpipe" is 4/4, so it looks like a reel. The difference is that a hornpipe is played with a dotted rhythm on beats 1 and 3 so that it swings. Hornpipes are also played slower than reels. They are often written with a "straight rhythm" as above, because a dotted rhythm throughout is somewhat visually overwhelming.

Exercise: Up and Down the Arpeggio/Hornpipe Rhythm

In this exercise you can see how the dotted rhythm works to give the hornpipe its swingy feel. This exercise also provides an opportunity to practice the finger patterns for each of the arpeggiated passages in this tune, in order to begin to develop muscle memory for each pattern.

Exercise: Bow Division

The dotted rhythm of the hornpipe can lead fiddlers to become stuck in the top part (tip) of the bow, since the dotted eighth notes tend to fall on down bows, while their shorter counterpart, the sixteenth notes, are up bows. Try the exercise below to support fluid bow movement.

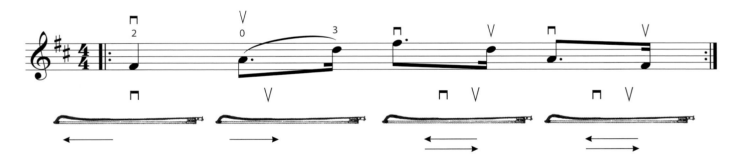

Exercise: The Pendulum

Imagine that your left arm in playing position is a pendulum. When playing on the E-string, the left elbow hangs in a neutral position so that it is pointing straight down at the floor. Now try moving your elbow slightly to the right (toward your rib cage) in increasing degree, as you imagine bringing your fingers to the D and G strings. When playing on the lower strings, this movement helps to bring your rounded fingers to the string so there is no strain on the hand and wrist. Try the exercise below without the bow, moving the right elbow slightly to the right with each string change. When you are ready, add the bow!

Buckskin Reel

Andy Dejarlis (Métis Reel)

"Buckskin Reel" is a very popular tune on the Canadian prairies and one of my personal favourites.

Exercise: Accent and Bow Division (Three-Note Slur)

For this exercise, start in the middle of the bow and move the bow quickly to a few inches from the tip. For the up bow slur, use the same amount of bow so that after playing the three slurred notes, you are back in the middle of the bow again. Moving your bow quickly on the first note creates an accent, or emphasis on this note. An accent provides a musical counterbalance to the slurred notes, giving texture or lilt to the melody.

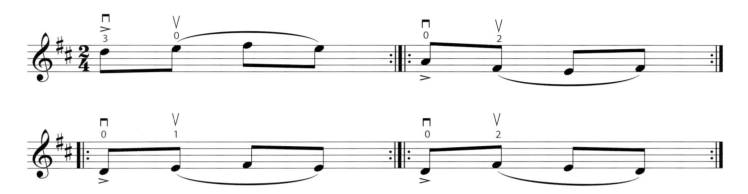

Exercise: Preparing For a Double Stop

While you are playing the first note, move finger 1 into place so that it is ready to go for the double stop. Keep in mind that for double stops, the fingers of the left hand do not need to press the strings down any harder than for a single note. The same is true of the bow—no extra pressure is needed—so try to maintain a relaxed left and right hand as you practice this exercise.

Exercise: C♯ Finger Placement on the G String

Bar 21 of "Buckskin Reel" introduces C♯ on the G string. To play this note, bring your left elbow under the violin so the fingers of your left hand are curled over the G string (as in The Pendulum exercise on page 69). Keeping finger 3 rounded, extend it so that it reaches *above* the tape (toward your nose) and sits on the string on the fingertip. You can find the precise spot for this note by using a tuner and if you like, marking the correct spot with a small piece of tape or a small sticker. It will be important to get your left elbow and finger 3 ready in advance of the note. Try the following exercises to get comfortable with C♯ on the G string.

Coming soon:

Once Upon A String Fiddle Method
Volume 2